Clinic
I've Seen Heaven and

By Jenny Sharkey

MW00928259

© 2013

All Rights Reserved. No part of this publication may be reproduced in any form or by any means, including scanning, photocopying, or otherwise without prior written permission of the copyright holder.

Disclaimer and Terms of Use: The Author and Publisher has strived to be as accurate and complete as possible in the creation of this book, notwithstanding the fact that she does not warrant or represent at any time that the contents within are accurate due to the rapidly changing nature of the Information Age. While all attempts have been made to verify information provided in this publication, the Author and Publisher assumes no responsibility for errors, omissions, or contrary interpretation of the subject matter herein. Any perceived slights of specific persons, peoples, or organizations are unintentional. In practical advice books, like anything else in life, there are no guarantees.

First Printing, 2012

Printed in the United States of America

Dedication

Dedicated to all those children

(young and old) who are yet to find

their home with the Father.

"Trust in God; trust also in me.

In my Father's house are many rooms;

If it were not so, I would have told you.

I am going there to prepare a place for you."

— Jesus in John 14:2

FOREWORD

Ian McCormack's story is profoundly moving, and completely credible. Although I am familiar with Ian's story, I found that reading this short book caused me to question again the ultimate purpose and destiny of my own life. Hopefully, other readers will be prompted to ask the same questions.

As an experienced General Practitioner, I have no doubt that Ian died following multiple stings from Box Jellyfish. The Box Jellyfish is one of the most dangerous venomous creatures in the world. Death from Box Jellyfish stings can occur within five minutes. Death is due to respiratory failure caused by paralysis of the respiratory centre in the brain, or to direct effects on the heart causing electrical conduction disturbances and paralysis of the cardiac muscle. Patients who have been stung by Box Jellyfish frequently become unconscious before leaving the water.

In my opinion Ian McCormack sustained a cardiac arrest, due to the toxic effects of Box Jellyfish stings. No blame is attached to his death, since a considerable time had elapsed before the antitoxin could be administered to Ian in hospital, making the prognosis extremely poor.

Ian's account of Jesus Christ, Heaven and Hell are completely in accord with the Biblical descriptions. In fact, like all supernatural events, the truth of these events should be checked against the truth of the Scriptures, as the Bereans did (Acts 17:11)*.

Ian later became an ordained minister in 1991, and has travelled widely all over the world speaking about his experience. Ian has made it his lifetime's goal to see as many people as possible end up in heaven, rather than hell, which is the reason for his travelling. His motive is not financial.

After hearing Ian speak, he so greatly impressed me that I co-authored two books on Near Death Experiences, and I now travel widely speaking on Near Death Experiences myself. I sincerely hope that as readers are confronted with the reality of heaven and hell, that they not only ensure their own destiny in heaven, but also encourage others to do the same.

Richard Kent

(Dr Richard Kent is a retired medical doctor, and is now an ordained minister. He is the co-author of "The Final Frontier", and "Beyond the Final Frontier", which include 51 Near Death Accounts. Readers can find out about other Near Death Experiences, and about Dr Richard Kent and the registered UK charity from which he operates on his website: www.finalfrontier.org.uk.)

*For further biblical correlations please refer to the notes at the back of the book.

Contents

CHAPTER ONE: THE BIG O.E.

There is a way that seems right to a man

but in the end it leads to death.

— Proverbs 14:12

It was 1980 and I was 24 years old when I set out on an adventure that was to turn my life upside down. I had saved some money and was eager to travel and explore the world. My best friend and I decided to sell our worldly possessions and head out on a surfing safari, an 'endless summer' holiday.

I was born and raised in New Zealand, a beautiful island country in the Pacific region. My parents were schoolteachers, and because of this we moved towns often, relocating in various rural areas. I had two siblings and together we had enjoyed many of the privileges that New Zealand children take for granted, such as summer holidays at the beach. From a young age I revelled in the sea.

I completed a university degree in agriculture at Lincoln University and then worked for two years as a farm consultant with the New Zealand Dairy Board. I loved farming. I loved working in the outdoors, and spent as much time as possible in outdoor pursuits. Most of my weekends were spent diving, surfing, tramping, and pursuing all kinds of sports.

After two years of working, I got the urge to travel. It is common in New Zealand for young adults to travel abroad for some 'overseas experience'. It's a phenomenon fondly termed 'The Big O.E.' So off I went with my surfboard under my arm.

I initially flew to Sydney, Australia and surfed my way up the East Coast to Surfers Paradise. I travelled light and stayed in the cheapest accommodation I could find, while spending my days catching good waves at Dee Why, Fosters, Lennox Heads, Byron Bay and Burleigh Heads.

I hitchhiked up through the outback of Australia to Darwin and then carried on to Bali in Indonesia, where I surfed Kuta Reef and then took my chances surfing Uluwatu, an amazing left-hand reef break. I also visited a few Hindu and Buddhist temple sites before continuing on overland through Java.

As I travelled through Asia the people often asked me if I was a Christian, presumably because I was white skinned and obviously of European descent. The question challenged me because I had been brought up in a Christian family, but I wasn't sure if I should call myself a Christian.

I was raised as an Anglican and attended the "Church of England". At the age of 14 years I was confirmed in the church. I would pray as a child, and went to 'Sunday school' and 'youth group', and yet I'd never really had a personal experience with God. I didn't feel as though I knew him.

I remember coming out of the church on the day of my confirmation quite disillusioned. Nothing seemed to have happened – nothing was changed as a result of participating in this religious experience. My heart was full of questions, so I asked my mother if God had ever spoken personally to her. She turned to me and said "God does speak and he is real". Then she shared how she had cried out to God in a time of tragedy and he had answered her. So I asked her why God hadn't ever spoken to me. I vividly remember her answer; "Often it takes a tragedy to humble us so that we will turn to God. Men by nature tend to be quite proud". I retorted, "I'm not that kind of person, I'm not proud". But when I reflect on it, I was very proud.

My mother said, "I'm not going to force you to come to church. But remember this one thing. Whatever you do in life, wherever you go, no matter how far you think you've gone away from God, remember this one thing; if you're in trouble and in need, cry out to God from your heart and he will hear you. He will really hear you and forgive you". I remembered those words. They stuck in my mind. But I decided that rather than be a hypocrite I wouldn't go back to church because I had never really had an experience with God. Christianity was basically just religion to me and void of relationship.

I travelled on up through Java, Singapore, Tiomen Island and into Malaysia, then onto Colombo in Sri Lanka with a Dutch woman I had met up with. Once there, I made my way up the coast to surf Arugum Bay. After a month of awesome waves my visa was running out so I returned to Colombo.

I befriended some Tamil people in Colombo who welcomed me into their home and family life. One time while I was staying with them we all travelled to the hidden city of Katragarma. While I was at this sacred city I had my first supernatural experience. As I was looking at a carved idol I actually saw its lips move. I was deeply disturbed by this experience and I wanted to leave the city as soon as I could.

As I continued to live with my Tamil friends, I observed that each day they would offer food to their household idol, the elephant god Garnesh. Some days they would clothe it, other days bath it in milk or water. It seemed strange to me that a person could believe a stone idol could be a god, as someone had obviously made it with their own hands. But looking at that stone statue one day I felt an evil yet powerful presence emanating from it. It surprised and intimidated me. Then into my mind these words came, "You shall have no other God but me, and you shall not bow down to any graven image or idol." Immediately I recognised this as one of the Ten Commandments found in the Bible (Exodus 20:4-5) and I began to reflect on these words that I had heard way back at Sunday school.

In my own way I was on a journey to find the 'meaning to life'. At times I considered myself an atheist, and at other times a 'free thinker'. These experiences made me think about supernatural things but I didn't have enough understanding of them to interpret them. I wanted to experience everything that life had to offer, and at that time my philosophy was simply to live life as fully as I could. In those years I never wore a watch. I lived in a timeless zone of sunrises and sunsets.

I eventually returned to Arugam Bay where I was excited to get a crewing position on a 27-metre schooner called the "Constellation". We sailed out of Sri Lanka in the middle of the night en route for Africa and twenty-six days later we arrived in Port Louis Harbour on the island of Mauritius.

I spent several weeks living in Tamarin Bay in Mauritius among the local Creole fishermen and surfers. Hashish (Marijuana) gave us a common bond and they accepted me into their lives and taught me to night dive on the outer reefs. Night diving is an incredible experience. The crayfish come out at night and you can blind them with your under water flashlight and just pick them up. The fish go to sleep at night and you only need to decide which one you want to spear for dinner. It was a fantastic sport and we would sell our catches to the local tourist hotel.

After several weeks of surfing to my heart's content on Tamarin's very fast left-hand reef break I was running out of money. So I headed to South Africa where I found a job teaching windsurfing and water-skiing. Amazingly they actually paid me to do this! I surfed Jeffrey's Bay and Elands Bay and visited some of South Africa's world famous wildlife reservations.

My desire was to travel over land through Africa up into Europe, but my plans were completely changed when I heard from New Zealand that my younger brother was planning to get married. I wanted to be at his wedding so I made the decision to return to New Zealand via Reunion Island, Mauritius and Australia.

At my stopover in Reunion I found an amazing surf break called St Leu where I had some great waves to myself. Then I headed on to Mauritius. It was March 1982 and I'd been travelling now for nearly two years, often sleeping in a tent on beaches and living like a nomad. It was time to return home.

CHAPTER TWO: THE BOX JELLYFISH

All the days ordained for me

were written in your book

before one of them came to be.

– Psalm 139:16 (NIV)

Back in Mauritius again for a few weeks, I rented a house, reconnected with my Creole friends, and spent my time surfing and night diving.

One evening, a week before I was due to leave for New Zealand, a diving friend came to my house and asked me to come out night diving with him. I walked out onto my verandah and saw a huge electrical storm raging out at sea. The white electric lightening flashes were illuminating the black sky. I turned to my friend Simon and asked, "Are you sure – have you seen the storm?" I was afraid the storm would bring up too much surf onto the reef and become dangerous. But Simon replied "It'll be okay, we'll go about five miles down the coast to a very beautiful part of the reef to dive tonight. You'll be amazed how beautiful it is."

In the end he talked me into it. It was about 11 o'clock at night. I got all my gear, jumped in the boat and off we all went - Simon, another local diver, a boat boy, and myself. We rowed down the coast to the spot that Simon had talked about. We were about half a mile off the actual island. The boat was sitting in the inner lagoon, and we were going to dive on the outer part of the reef where it drops away steeply into the ocean. It really was as beautiful as Simon had said it would be.

We dived in. I went up the reef and my two friends went down the reef. Normally we stick together but for some reason we got separated. I was looking for crayfish when my flashlight beam picked out a strange sea creature in the dark water. It looked like a squid. Curious, I swam closer to it and actually reached out my hand and grabbed it. I had my diving gloves on and it squeezed through my fingers like a jellyfish. As it floated away I watched it, intrigued, as it was a very odd looking jellyfish. It had what appeared to be a squid's bell-shaped head, but its back was box shaped and it had very unusual, transparent, finger like tentacles stretching way out behind it. I'd never seen that type of jellyfish before, but I turned away from it and continued with my crayfish search.

As I turned my flashlight back onto the reef, suddenly something smashed into my forearm like a thousand volts of electricity. I swung around to see what it was. I had a short arm wetsuit on, so the only part of my body that wasn't covered by a wetsuit was my forearms. Something had brushed past me and stung me with incredible intensity. It was like standing on wet concrete, bare foot, and resting your hand right up against the electrical mains. I recoiled from it in fright, and searched frantically with my flashlight to find out what it was, or where it was, but I couldn't see what had hit me.

Maybe something had bitten me, or I'd cut myself on the reef? I looked down at my arm to see if there was any blood, but there was nothing, just a throbbing pain. I rubbed it, which turned out to be one of the worst things I could have done as it served to rub the poison into my bloodstream. By now the pain seemed to be numbing out a bit so I thought, "I'll just get a crayfish and then I'll go back and ask the boy at the boat what it was." I didn't want to get paranoid; I knew it was very important for my own safety as a diver not to panic.

So I went to get a crayfish. As I was diving under again I saw these same jellyfish creatures that I'd seen a few minutes ago. Two of them were slowly, eerily, pulsating towards me with their long tentacles swirling behind them. Out of the corner of my eye I saw their tentacles brush past my arm. As they touched my arm, I was again jolted by a startling electric shock. It just about knocked me for a six in the water. I suddenly realised what it was that had hit me the first time!

I knew from my lifesaving experience that some jellyfish are incredibly poisonous. As a child I had hay fever and had such bad allergic reactions that if I got stung by a bee my leg would swell up like a balloon. Now I began feeling alarmed because I'd had two separate stings from these jellyfish. I broke the surface of the water, gasping for air, and lifted my head to look for the boat.

The storm clouds were settling in and making everything dark. I could just make the boat out further down the reef. I put my arm behind my back to get it out of the water. I didn't want it to be stung again. Then I began to swim in the direction of the reef, trying to fight off the terror I was feeling. As I swam I felt something slide over my back and then another huge shock pulsed through my arm. Looking round I saw tentacles falling off. I'd been stung by a third one!

I put my flashlight back into the water to keep an eye on the reef and to my horror my flashlight beam went straight down through a soup of these jellyfish. I thought, "If one of these hits my face, I don't think I'll ever get back to the boat". So I put the flashlight up near my face and swam for all I was worth.

Finally I made it back to the boat where I desperately questioned the young boy in my best French and Creole, asking if he knew what the jellyfish were. He didn't know because he wasn't a diver, he just shook his head and he pointed to my friend Simon in the water. So I had to get back into the water and swim over to him.

I could see him underwater, so I flashed my light into his face to get his attention. He came up to the surface, and I exclaimed to him "I want to get out!" I put my head into the water to swim back to the boat and right in front of my face there was another jellyfish surging at me. I had to choose, it was either going to hit my face or my arm. So I lifted my arm up and took another agonising shock as I pushed it away. Then I struggled out on to the reef.

Two feet of water covered the actual reef. I stood there in my flippers and looked at my arm, which was by now swollen like a balloon with lesions across the top of the skin like burn blisters. It was as though I'd burnt it on the ring element of a stove right across where the tentacles had been dragged.

As I was looking at it, my friend Simon came walking across the reef in his flippers towards me. He was wearing a full wetsuit, as they all did because they were brought up in the tropics and the water felt cold to them. He looked at my arm, and then he looked at me. He asked breathlessly, "How many? How many times have you been stung?" I answered, "Four I think." He said, "Invisible? Was it transparent?" I replied, "Yeah, it looks invisible." Simon hung his head down and swore. He said "One sting and you're finished, just one!" He put his flashlight up to his face and I could see written there the seriousness of the situation. I said "Well, what am I doing with four of them on my arm then?"

Simon was panicking, and I was panicking because he had been diving for years and I trusted his knowledge of the sea world. "You've got to get to the hospital." He said, "Aller, aller, vite." The main hospital was 15 miles away, it was the middle of the night and I was half a mile out to sea on a reef. I could hear him say "go" but I felt paralysed standing there. He was trying to get me back into the boat. As he dragged me in I realised that my right arm was literally paralysed and I couldn't lift it up out of the water. At that point, as I was trying to drag my arm up out of the water into the boat a fifth jellyfish swam across it and added another lesion to my already disfigured forearm.

In my heart I thought, "What have I done to deserve this?" Then I got a flashback of my sin. I knew instantly what I'd done wrong. There were plenty of things I had done to deserve this. You don't get away with anything.

My two friends lifted the boat over the reef with me in it. It was ripping the bottom. It was a wooden boat, and the boat was their livelihood, so I knew the situation was very serious for them to be doing that. They lifted the boat over into the lagoon and were swimming, trying to push the boat to get it going. I said, "Come with me!" But they replied, "No, it's too heavy, get the young boy to take you ashore". So this young kid was pushing the boat to shore with a pole.

I felt like I was on fire. I could feel the poison going through my blood stream and it punched at something under my arm. A lymph gland was being hit. It was becoming increasingly difficult for me to breathe into my right lung. My right lung was being constricted by my wetsuit so I undid my wetsuit with my left arm, peeled it off and put on my trousers while I could still move. My mouth was dry and I sat there dripping with perspiration. I could feel the poison moving. I could feel a sharp pain in my back as if someone had hit me in the kidneys. I was trying not to move, trying not to panic. We were only half way to shore and the poison was already pulsating and moving through my blood system.

I didn't know or care what direction my blood went in until that night, but at that moment I became really interested in which way my blood circulated!

The poison was now numbing out the whole of my right leg, and I had enough common sense to know that if it got down that leg and back up to my heart or my brain, then I was in serious trouble. As I was coming to shore, my vision was blurring. I was finding it difficult to focus.

We reached the shore and I stood up to get out of the boat and my right leg crumbled underneath me. I fell right onto the crayfish in the bottom of the boat. The young boy stood back a bit shocked, and then he motioned for me to put my arm around him. I threw my arm around his neck and just held on. He dragged me out of the boat and then up the beach on the coral sand. He got me up onto the main road.

It was about midnight. The place was desolate - no cars, no nothing. I was holding on to the young boy wondering how on earth I was going to get from there to the hospital at such a late time of the night. I was so weak in my right leg that I sat down on the tarmac. The young boy tried to help me but in the end he started pointing to the ocean again saying, "My brothers, I need to get them". I said, "No, stay here and help me." I knew the others could safely swim in from the reef because the jellyfish were on the outside of the reef. But he took off, and I was left alone on the side of the road in the middle of the night. Hope drained from me and I lay down to rest.

CHAPTER THREE: THE ENDURANCE TEST

When my spirit grows faint within me

It is you who know my way

In the path where I walk

Men have hidden a snare for me

Look to my right and see;

No one is concerned for me

I have no refuge

No one cares for my life

– Psalm 142:3,4 (NIV)

Tiredness overwhelmed me as I stared up into the stars. I was just about to close my eyes and go to sleep, when I heard a clear voice speak to me, and say "Ian, if you close your eyes you shall never awake again". I looked around expecting to see a man standing there but I saw no-one. It startled me and I shook off the sleepiness and thought, "What am I doing? I can't go to sleep here, I need to get to a hospital, I need to get anti-toxins, and I need to get help. If I go to sleep here I may actually never wake up."

So I tried to stand again. I was able to hobble slowly down the road and I found a couple of taxis parked at a petrol station next to a restaurant. I limped over to the taxis and begged the drivers to take me to the hospital. The men in the cars looked at me and said, "How much money will you pay us?" So I said, "I haven't got any money" - speaking out loud to myself. Then I realised what a foolish thing it was to admit to these men that I had no money. I could have lied, but I didn't, I just told the truth. I had no money.

And the three drivers just laughed, "You're drunk, you're crazy". They turned around, lit their cigarettes and started to walk off.

Then I heard a clear voice again say "Ian, are you willing to beg for your life?" I sure was! And I even knew how to do it. I had lived in South Africa long enough. I'd seen the black men cup their hands and bow their heads to the white men and say, "Yes'm boss, yes'm marsta."

It was very easy for me to get down on my knees because my right leg was already paralysed, and my left leg was very wobbly. I was leaning up against the car so I just slipped down on to my knees and cupped my hands. Lowering my head I begged for my life. I was nearly crying. I knew that if I didn't get to hospital soon I wasn't going anywhere. If these guys didn't have compassion and love in their heart for me, and mercy towards me, I would have died right there in front of them.

So I begged and pleaded with them for my life. With my head bent I watched their feet. Two of them just walked away, but I could see one young man moving his feet in indecision. It seemed to go on for an unbearably long time, but then he come over and picked me up. He didn't speak but he helped me up, put me in the car and drove off.

Half way to the hospital however, he changed his mind. He demanded, "What hotel you stay in white man?" I replied that I didn't live in a hotel but in a bungalow at Tamarin Bay. He thought I had lied to him and became angry – suspecting that he might not get any money from me after all. "How will I get my money?" he retorted. I answered, "I'll give you all the money I've got!" When your life's at stake, money means nothing. I said "I'll give you any money you want if you can get me to hospital. I'll give you it all." But he didn't believe me.

So he changed his mind and took me to a big tourist hotel. He said "I'll drop you here; I'm not going to take you." I pleaded with him to take me but he leaned over, undid my safety belt and opened the door. "Get out!" he demanded. But I couldn't get out, I could barely move. So he had to push me out.

My legs caught on the doorsill so he lifted them up and thrust them out, slammed the door and drove off. I lay there, and thought, "This world stinks. I've seen death, hatred, violence; this is hell, this place is hell on earth. This is a filthy, sick world we live in." I lay there in utter hopelessness. I thought, "What's the point of even trying to get to hospital? If your number's up let it go, just die."

Then my grandfather came to mind. He went through the First and Second World Wars. He'd been to Gallipoli and had fought in Egypt against Rommel. I remembered this and thought how my Granddad had survived two world wars and here was his grandson giving up because five miserable jellyfish had stung him! The thought of him revived my courage and I resolved not to die without doing whatever I could to get help. Using my one remaining working arm I tried to drag myself towards the hotel entrance. I could see some lights on. To my amazement the security guards were doing the rounds and their flashlights spotted me groveling along in the dirt.

A man came running over. I looked up and recognised him to be one of my drinking friends. He was a black guy called Daniel, a big lovable man. He came running up to me and asked, "What's wrong with you? Are you drunk? Are you stoned? What's wrong with you?" I pulled up my sweatshirt to show him my arm and he could see all the blisters and the swollenness. He scooped me up in his arms and ran.

It was like having an angel pick me up. He ran inside, past the hotel swimming pool and dropped me into a cane chair. About three metres away the Chinese hotel owners were playing mahjong and drinking. All the tourists had gone to bed, the bar was closed but they were still gambling.

Daniel dropped me there and disappeared into the darkness again. I wondered where he had gone but then I realised that a black man couldn't speak to a Chinese man in this country unless he is asked to speak. I was going to have to try and communicate to these Chinese men myself. So I pulled up my sleeve and showed them my swollen and blistered limb. I said, "I need to go to 'Quartre Bonne' hospital immediately, I've been stung by five jellyfish." I even used some Chinese. They laughed.

12

One of the young men got up and said "Oh white boy, heroin no good for you, only old men take the Opium." He thought I was on drugs because I showed him my arm and from that distance it looked like I had injected myself.

I was becoming furious and frustrated by this. I sat there trying to keep myself calm, because I knew that if I got too excited the poison would move more rapidly through my blood system. My right hand started to shake. It was twitching strangely between my knuckles, in spasms. The twitching came up my arm and into my face and my teeth began chattering.

Soon my whole body, every muscle, started to twitch and contract with the death shakes. I was literally leaving my seat with each contraction as the poison was reacting with my muscles. The Chinese men came running over and three men tried to hold me down. They couldn't contain me; I was throwing them off.

When I came out of this incredible shaking a deadly cold crept over my bone marrow. I could actually see a darkness creeping over the inner part of my bone. It was like death creeping over me. I knew my body was dying, right before my eyes. I was incredibly cold.

The men started putting blankets all over me trying to keep me warm. One of them tried to pour milk down my throat, presuming I had swallowed toxin. I could see one vehicle in the hotel car park. I knew which man it belonged as he had often driven past me and sounded his horn when I had hitchhiked from place to place. I pleaded with him to take me in his car to the hospital but he refused. He wanted to wait for the ambulance to come. I was so mad I wanted to hit him, but I couldn't move either of my arms. I considered head-butting him but I was aware that the adrenaline it would use might kill me.

In a short while the ambulance arrived and out of nowhere Daniel appeared with another security man. They picked me up in their arms and jogged with me back outside. I realised then that Daniel had gone straight to the switchboard and phoned the hospital himself.

The ambulance came screaming in with its headlights sweeping the car park, did a U-turn in front of the hotel, and took off again! The ambulance driver was from a black hospital, so when there was no one at the front of the Chinese hotel to collect he obviously thought he had his instructions wrong.

So there I was, desperate, half way to the gates, and I could see the ambulance disappearing around the corner. I tried to whistle but my mouth was so parched couldn't get a sound out. Daniel saw what I was trying to do and he whistled as loud as he could. It ricocheted off the wall and down the road.

The ambulance driver must have had his window down because the red brake lights came on and to my great relief he backed up. The ambulance was an old Renault 4 with a front seat taken out and a camp stretcher put in its place. That's it boys, that's the ambulance! I wasn't worried. I didn't care what took me there.

The driver didn't even get out of the ambulance. He leaned over, opened the door and Daniel dropped me in on the stretcher. No, "How's your mother? How are you? Do you want a blanket? What's wrong with you?" He was just the driver and off he went. I was trying not to close my eyes, knowing that I had to stay awake until I got some anti-toxins. If only I could stay alive until I reached the hospital.

CHAPTER FOUR: THE LORD'S PRAYER

Our Father who is in heaven

Holy be your name

Your kingdom come

Your will be done

On earth as it is in heaven

Give us this day our daily bread

And forgive us our sins

As we forgive those who sin against us

Lead us not into temptation

But deliver us from evil

For yours is the kingdom

The power and the glory

Forever and Ever

Amen

(Adapted from Matthew 6: 9-13)

We were half way to the hospital and the Renault was climbing a hill. My feet were going up in the air and the poison in my blood was starting to rush straight to my brain. I started seeing a picture of a little snowy-headed boy, and then I saw another flash of an older boy with snowy white hair.

I was looking at this picture thinking, "Gee, he's got white hair," and it suddenly occurred to me that I was looking at myself, that I was seeing my life go before me. It was a frightening experience watching these pictures of my life in front of me like a video playing, clear as crystal with my eyes wide open. I looked and thought, "I've heard about this, and I've even read about it. People say just before they die their life flashes before them."

My thoughts were racing. "I'm too young to die, why did I go diving? What an idiot. I should have stayed at home." Now I knew I was confronted with imminent death. I could hardly hear my heart beat and I lay there wondering what would happen if I died? Is there anything after I die? Where would I go if I died?

Then I saw a clear vision of my mother. It was as though she was speaking out those words she had spoken so long ago; "Ian, no matter how far from God you are, no matter what you've done wrong, if you cry out to God from your heart, he will hear you and he will forgive you."

In my heart I was thinking, "Do I believe there is a God? Am I going to pray?" I'd almost become a devout atheist. I didn't believe anybody. Yet, I was confronted by this vision of my mother. Little did I know that my mother had been woken in the early hours of the morning in New Zealand at the same time I was going through this dying experience. God had shown her my blood shot eyes and said to her, "your eldest son Ian is nearly dead. Pray for him now." So she had been praying for me at that very moment that I lay dying in the ambulance.

Now of course her prayers couldn't save my soul, she couldn't get me to heaven, but I knew at that moment that I needed to pray. Only I didn't know what to pray or who to pray to. Which god should I pray to? Buddha? Kali? Shiva? There are thousands of them. Yet I didn't see Buddha or Krishna or some other god or man standing there, I saw my mother - and my mother followed Jesus Christ.

I wondered what I should pray. I hadn't prayed for years. What do you pray at this point? What's the prayer if you're about to die?" Then I remembered that as a child my mother taught us the 'Lord's prayer'. "Our Father who is in heaven, holy be your name, your kingdom come, your will be done on earth as it is in heaven... "I knew it as a child – I used to race my siblings each night to say it the fastest!

That was the only prayer I knew. I started to pray it, but I couldn't remember it. It was as though the poison that had rushed to my head had inhibited my thinking ability. It was closing my mind down. It was terrifying. I had relied so much on my mind and my intellect and now suddenly it was dying on me. Mental blank. Zero.

As I was lying there I remember my mother saying that you don't pray from your head, you pray from your heart, so I asked God to help me pray. Immediately this prayer came up from deep inside me, from my spirit. I prayed, "Forgive us our sins." Then I went on "God, I ask you to forgive my sins, but I have done so many things wrong. I know they're wrong, my conscience tells me they're wrong. If you can forgive me all my sins, and I don't know how you can do it - I've got no idea how you can forgive them but please forgive me of my sins". And I meant it. I wanted to wipe the slate clean, start again. "God forgive me."

As I prayed that, I got another part of the prayer. "Forgive those who have sinned against you." I understood that that meant I had to forgive those who had hurt me. I thought, "Well I don't hold grudges. There are heaps of people that have ripped me off and back-stabbed me and said bad things against me - I forgive them."

Then I heard this question, "Will you forgive the Indian that pushed you out of the car and the Chinese men that wouldn't take you to the hospital?" I thought, "You must be joking! I had other plans for them!" But no more of the prayer would come. I knew I was in a catch 22 position. I thought, "Okay, I'll forgive them. If you can forgive me, I can forgive them. I will forgive them. I'll never lay a hand on them."

The next part of the prayer came to me, "Your will be done." I had done my own thing for the last 20 years. I said, "God, I don't even know what your will is - I know it's not to do evil things, but I've got no idea what your will is.

If I come through this, I will find out your will for my life and I'll do it. I'll make a point of following you whole-heartedly if I come through this".

I didn't understand it at the time, but that was my prayer for salvation. Not from my head, but from my heart, asking "God forgive me for my wickedness and evil-doing. God cleanse me. I forgive all those that have hurt me. And Jesus Christ, I'll do your will - your will be done. I will follow you." I had prayed a sinner's prayer, a repentant prayer to God, and praying that prayer was pivotal to everything else that happened to me.

An incredible peace came over my heart. It seemed as though fear fell off me, the fear of what was coming. I was still dying, I knew that, but I was at peace about it. I'd made peace with my Maker. I knew it, I knew for the first time that I had relationship with God and I was actually hearing him. I'd never heard him before but now I was hearing him speaking to me. No one else could have told me the Lord's Prayer.

CHAPTER FIVE: THE FINAL RELEASE

You can enter God's Kingdom

only through the narrow gate.

The highway to hell is broad and its gate is wide

for the many who chose the easy way.

But the gateway to life is small,

and the road is narrow,

and only a few

ever find it.

– Matthew 7:13,14 (NLT)

The ambulance turned off the road in to the hospital. Finally I had made it! The driver lifted me into a wheelchair and ran me through to the emergency area. A nurse began to take my blood pressure. As I was sitting there watching the nurse she looked at the gauge and then she hit it. I thought, "What kind of hospital is this?" It was an old World War Two army hospital which the British had deserted and given it to the Creole people. It looked like it was built in 1945 and had had very little maintenance since then. It was filthy and decrepit and yet there I was.

The nurse hit the gauge again and I realised there was nothing wrong with the machine, the problem was that my heart wasn't beating strongly enough to register. She ripped off the gauge and rummaged through the cupboard, trying to find another one that looked newer. She pulled one out, slapped it on, opened it up and started pumping. She looked at me, and then looked at the machine. My eyes were open, but I knew she was wondering why they were open. With this kind of blood pressure your eyes shouldn't be open. I was desperately hanging on. I was hanging on for all I was worth. I was fighting with all my strength to stay alive.

So the ambulance driver, realising the situation was desperate, ripped the gauge off my arm and ran me through to the doctors. Two Indian doctors were sitting there, both of them half-asleep, heads down. One asked in French: "What's your name? Where do you live? How old are you?" He was a young doctor and he didn't even look at me. I looked over to the older doctor. He had a bit of gray hair and I thought, "He's been around for a few years, he might know how to help me." So I waited.

The young doctor stopped talking and looked up. I didn't even bother looking at him but waited for the old man to lift his head up. He looked up. I wasn't sure if I had enough strength left to speak. I locked into his eyes and I gave him the heaviest look I could muster. I whispered "I am about to die, I need anti-toxins right now". He didn't move. I didn't take my eyes off him, he was just staring straight back into them.

The nurse came in with a piece of paper. The older doctor looked at it, looked at me, and jumped. I could see him screw it up in disgust. He pushed the ambulance driver out of the way, grabbed the wheelchair himself and started racing me down the corridor. I could hear him yelling out something but all the noise became muffled to me. My senses were beginning to fade.

The doctor ran into a room with bottles and medical equipment in it. Next minute I was surrounded by nurses, doctors and orderlies. At long last, something was happening. A nurse turned my arm over and put in a drip feed. The doctor was up near my face saying, "I don't know if you can hear me son but we're going to try and save your life. Keep your eyes open... come on son, fight the poison. Try and keep awake, we're putting dextrose in for dehydration."

The doctor was saying to the nurses, "Anti-toxins to counteract the poison" in his Oxford English. A nurse jabbed a needle in one side and another nurse was on the other side, jabbing. I couldn't feel them but I could see them doing it. Another nurse knelt by my feet, slapping my hand as hard as she could. I was thinking, "What is she doing?" But I didn't care, just shove the needles in!

A nurse behind me was filling a huge syringe, like a horse syringe. She was squeezing the air out of it. She tried to stick it in my arm but no vein came up. So she lifted my skin up, put the needle in and started pushing the liquid in. It filled up my vein like a small balloon. I could see how nervous she was because the needle was inside the vein and it looked like it was shaking so much that it would tear my vein open.

She left that needle in and someone passed her another needle. Again, it blew the vein up. The nurse looked at the doctor and asked him, "Another one?" The doctor nodded. So she tried another one. A nurse was now trying to massage it in but the vein was actually rolling off her thumb. She couldn't get the anti-toxin into the blood, it was just not moving.

My heart was obviously not pumping around enough blood. My veins were collapsing. I'd done veterinary science in my degree so I understood basic physiology and anatomy. I understood what was going on, but I couldn't do anything about it. I understood that I was slipping into a comatose state.

I was totally paralysed, and my heart was barely pumping. As I was watching the needles, I felt myself slipping further and further away. I couldn't communicate any more, I couldn't say a thing, but I could still hear everything that was being said about and around me.

I had no idea that what I'd been stung by was a box jellyfish or a Sea-wasp. The box jellyfish exudes the second deadliest venom known to man. Being stung only once has killed up to 60 people in Darwin alone over the last 20 years. For six months of the year they put up a skull and cross bones sign on the beaches in Darwin to prevent bathers from going into the water to swim. I had enough toxins in me to kill me five times over. Normally a person dies within fifteen minutes of the initial sting and I didn't have it just on a muscle, I had it right across my veins.

The doctor was telling me not to be afraid but I could see the paranoia in his eyes. I was lifted onto a bed with my drip feed. The drip feed they had put in my veins was bringing liquid back into my body and I was starting to perspire on my forehead. The doctor was wiping it from my face, but then he walked off for a few minutes. As I lay there I could feel the sweat dripping into my eyes like tears, and it started to blur my vision.

I knew I had to keep my eyes open. I willed the doctor to come back and wipe my face but he didn't return. I tried to speak but my lips would not move. I tried to tilt my head but my head wouldn't move. I flicked some out with my eyelids. I kept squeezing my eyelids shut. It worked a little, and then all of a sudden I sighed, like a sigh of relief and I knew something had happened.

CHAPTER SIX: THE DARKNESS

Light has come into the world,

but men loved darkness instead of light

because their deeds were evil.

– John 3:19 (NIV)

Many... will be cast into outer darkness,

where there will be weeping and gnashing of teeth.

– Matthew 8:12 (NLT)

I knew there was a release; the battle to stay alive was over. I knew I'd gone somewhere, it wasn't like closing your eyes and going to sleep, I knew I'd actually gone somewhere. For the previous 20 minutes in the hospital I had been feeling like I was floating away and yet when I closed my eyes, I wasn't floating away any more - I was gone.

The Bible says in Ecclesiastes, that when a man dies his spirit returns to God who gave it and his body returns to the dust from which it came. Well, I knew my spirit had left, I had gone somewhere, and yet I didn't know I was dead.

I seemed to arrive in a huge, broad place like a cavernous hall of pitch-black darkness. I was standing up. It was as if I had woken up from a bad dream in someone else's house, and was wondering where everyone had gone. I was trying to find the light switch, and I couldn't seem to find it. I wondered why the doctor had turned the lights out. I was trying to touch something, reaching for the wall lamp but I couldn't find it. Then I realised I couldn't find my bed. I was moving around but I wasn't bumping into anything – I couldn't get a fix on anything tangible.

I strained to see where I was - trying to orient myself to these new surroundings. It was so dark I couldn't see my hand in front of my face and it was bitterly cold. I lifted my hand up to find out how much I could see. I lifted it to where my face was and it went straight through where my face should have been. It was a terrifying experience. I knew right there and then, I was myself, Ian McCormack, standing there, but without a physical body. I had the sensation and the feeling that I had a body, but I couldn't touch it.

I was a spiritual being, and my physical body had died, but I was very much alive, and very much aware that I had arms and legs and a head, but I could no longer touch them. God is a spirit, an invisible spiritual being, and we are created in his image.

"Where on earth am I?" I thought. As I was standing there in the darkness, I sensed the most horrifying cold dread come over me. Maybe you've walked down a lonely street at night, or you've come home by yourself in the dark and you've felt as though there is someone looking at you. Ever felt that? Well I began to sense evil encroaching on me in the darkness. The darkness seemed invasive. I knew I was being watched. A terrifying encroaching evil seemed to pervade the air around me.

Slowly I became aware that there were other people moving around me, in the same predicament as I was. Without my saying a word out loud, they began to answer my thoughts. From the darkness I heard a voice screaming at me: "Shut up!" As I backed away from that one another yelled at me, "You deserve to be here!" My arms came up to protect myself and I thought, "Where am I?" and a third voice shouted, "You're in hell. Now shut up." I was terrified – afraid to move or breathe or speak. I realised that maybe I did deserve this place.

People sometimes have this strange picture of hell being party time. I used to think that. I thought that in hell you would get to do all the things there that you're not supposed to do on earth. That is so far from the reality of it.

The place I was in was the most frightening place I've ever been. The people there could not do anything that their wicked hearts wanted to do. They couldn't do anything. And there's no boasting. There's nothing to talk about when you know that judgment is coming.

There is no relationship to time in that place. The people there couldn't tell what time it was. They couldn't tell whether they had been there ten minutes, ten years or 10,000 years. They had no relationship to time. It was a frightening place.

The Bible says that there are two kingdoms, the Kingdom of Darkness, which is ruled by Satan, and the Kingdom of Light. The book of Jude indicates that the place of darkness was actually prepared for angels that disobeyed God, not for people, ever. It was the scariest and the most terrifying place I have ever been in. I would never wish that even my worst enemy went to hell.

I had no idea how to get out of that place. How do you ever get out of hell? But I had already prayed, and I was wondering why I'd gone there, because I'd prayed just before I died, and asked God to forgive me for my sins. I was weeping by now and I cried out to God, "Why am I here, I've asked you for forgiveness, why am I here? I've turned my heart to you, why am I here?"

Then a brilliant light shone upon me and literally drew me out of the darkness. The Bible says in the book of Isaiah that a great light has shined into the darkness, on those walking in the shadow of death, and has guided their feet into the paths of peace and righteousness. As I stood there an amazing beam of light pierced through the darkness from above me and shone on my face. This light began to encompass me and a sense of weightlessness overwhelmed me. I lifted off the ground and began to ascend up into this brilliant white light, like a speck of dust caught in a beam of sunlight.

CHAPTER SEVEN: THE LIGHT

For God, who said,

"Let there be light in the darkness,"

has made us understand that this light

is the brightness of the glory of God

that is seen in the face of Jesus.

– 2 Corinthians 4:6 (NIV)

As I looked up I could see I was being drawn into a large circular shaped opening far above me – a tunnel. I didn't want to look behind me in case I fell back into the darkness. I was very happy to be out of that darkness.

Upon entering the tunnel I could see that the source of the light was emanating from the very end of the tunnel. It looked unspeakably bright, as if it was the centre of the universe, the source of all light and power. It was more brilliant than the sun, more radiant than any diamond, brighter than a laser beam. Yet you could look right into it.

As I looked I was literally drawn to it, drawn like a moth into the presence of a flame. I was being pulled through the air at an amazing speed towards the end of the tunnel – towards the source of the light.

As I was being translated through the air I could see successive waves of thicker intensity light break off the source and start travelling up the tunnel towards me. The first wave of light gave off an amazing warmth and comfort. It was as though the light wasn't just material in nature but was a 'living light' that transmitted an emotion. The light passed into me and filled me with a sense of love and acceptance.

Half way down another wave of light passed into me. This light gave off total and complete peace. I had looked for many years for 'peace of mind' but had only found fleeting moments of it. At school I had read from Keats to Shakespeare to try and get peace of mind. I had tried alcohol, I had tried education, I had tried sport, I had tried relationships with women, I had tried drugs, I tried everything I could think of to find peace and contentment in my life, and I'd never found it. Now from the top of my head to the base of my feet I found myself totally at peace.

In the darkness I hadn't been able to see my hands in front of my face but now as I looked to my right to my amazement there was my arm and hand – and I could see straight through them. I was transparent like a spirit, only my body was full of the same light that was shining on me from the end of the tunnel. It was as if I was full of light.

A third wave broke off the main source of light as I neared the end of the tunnel. This wave hit me and as it did total joy went through my being. It was so exciting that I knew that what I was about to see would be the most awesome experience in all my life.

My mind couldn't even conceive where I was going, and my words couldn't communicate what I saw. I came out of the end of the tunnel and seemed to be standing upright before the source of all the light and power. My whole vision was taken up with this incredible light. It looked like a white fire or a mountain of cut diamonds sparkling with the most indescribable brilliance. I immediately thought of it as aura, then as glory. I had seen pictures of Jesus with a little halo or small glow around his face yet this glory was all encompassing, overwhelming, awe inspiring.

Jesus died to rescue us from the place I'd just come from, he rose from the dead and ascended into heaven, and he is now seated at the right-hand of the Father, and is glorified, surrounded by light and in him there is no darkness. He is the King of Glory, the Prince of Peace, the Lord of Lords and the King of all the Kings.

I saw at that moment what I believe was the glory of the Lord. In the Old Testament, Moses went up Mount Sinai and saw the glory of the Lord.

When he came down his face shone so much with the glory of the Lord that he had to wear a veil so that the people wouldn't be afraid. He had seen the light of God, the glory of God. Paul was blinded by a glorious light on the road to Damascus, the glory of Jesus. And I was now standing there seeing this incredible light and glory.

As I stood there, questions began racing through my heart; "Is this just a force, as the Buddhists say, or karma or Yin and Yang? Is this just some innate power or energy source or could there actually be someone standing in there?" I was still questioning it all.

As I thought these thoughts a voice spoke to me from the centre of the light. It was the same voice that I had heard earlier in the evening. The voice said, "Ian, do you wish to return?" I was shaken to learn that there was someone in the centre of the light and whoever it was knew my name. It was as though the person could hear my inner thoughts as speech. I then thought to myself "Return, return – to where? Where am I?"

Quickly looking behind me I could see the tunnel dissipating back into darkness. I thought I must be in my hospital bed dreaming and I closed my eyes. "Is this real? Am I actually standing here, me, Ian, standing in real life here, is this real?" Then the Lord spoke again. "Do you wish to return?" I replied "If I am out of my body I don't know where I am, I wish to return." The response from this person was "If you wish to return Ian you must see in a new light."

The moment I heard the words "see in a new light," something clicked. I remembered being given a Christmas card, which said, "Jesus is the light of the world", and "God is light and there is no darkness in him." I had meditated upon those words at that time. I'd just come from darkness, and there was certainly no darkness here. I realised then that the light could be coming from Jesus, and if it was – then what was I doing here? I didn't deserve to be here.

CHAPTER EIGHT: THE WAVES OF LOVE

May you experience the love of Christ,

though it is so great you will

never fully understand it.

Then you will be filled with the fullness

of the life and power that comes from God

– Ephesians 3:19 (NLT)

So this was God! He is light. He knew my name and he knew the secret thoughts of my heart and mind. I thought, "If this is God then he must also be able to see everything I've ever done in my life."

I felt totally exposed and transparent before God. You can wear masks before other people but you can't wear a mask before God. I felt ashamed and undone and I thought, "They've made a mistake and brought the wrong person up. I shouldn't be here. I'm not a very good person. I should crawl under some rock or go back into the darkness where I belong."

As I began to slowly move back towards the tunnel a wave of light emanated forth from God and moved towards me. My first thought was that this light was going to cast me back into the pit, but to my amazement a wave of pure unconditional love flowed over me. It was the last thing I expected. Instead of judgement I was being washed with pure love.

Pure, unadulterated, clean, uninhibited, undeserved, love. It began to fill me up from the inside out, making my hands and body tingle until I staggered. I thought, "Perhaps God doesn't know all the things I've done wrong," so I proceeded to tell him about all the disgusting things I'd done under the cover of darkness. But it was as though he'd already forgiven me and the intensity of his love only increased. In fact, later God showed me that when I'd asked for forgiveness in the ambulance, it was then that he forgave me and washed my spirit clean from evil.

I found myself beginning to weep uncontrollably as the love became stronger and stronger. It was so clean and pure, no strings attached. I hadn't felt loved for years. The last time I remember being loved was by my mum and dad when I was at home, but I'd gone out into the big wide world and found out there's not too much love out there.

I'd seen things that I thought were love, but sex wasn't love, it just burnt you up. Lust was like a raging fire inside you, an uncontrollable desire that burnt you up from the inside out. Yet this love was healing my heart and I began to understand that there is incredible hope for humankind in this love. God's mercy is always extended before his judgement.

As I stood there, the waves of light stopped and I stood encased in pure light, filled with love. There was such stillness. I was so close I wondered if I could just step into the light that surrounded God and see him face to face. If I could only see him face to face I would know the truth. I was sick of hearing lies and deceptions. I wanted to know the truth. I had been everywhere to find the truth, and no one seemed to be able to tell me. I thought if I could step through and meet God face-to-face I would know the truth and the meaning to life.

Could I step in? There was no voice saying I couldn't. So, I stepped through, I put my best foot forward and stepped through the light. As I stepped into the light it was as if I'd come inside veils of suspended shimmering lights, like suspended stars or diamonds giving off the most amazing radiance. And as I walked through the light it continued to heal the deepest part of me, it was healing my broken inner man, wonderfully healing my broken heart.

I aimed for the brightest part of the light. Standing in the centre of the light stood a man with dazzling white robes reaching down to his ankles. I could see his bare feet. The garments were not man-made fabrics but were like garments of light. As I lifted my eyes up I could see the chest of a man with his arms outstretched as if to welcome me. I looked towards his face. It was so bright; it seemed to be about ten times brighter than the light I'd already seen. It made the sun look yellow and pale in comparison. It was so bright that I couldn't make out the features of his face, and as I stood there I began to sense that the light was emitting purity and holiness.

I knew that I was standing in the presence of Almighty God – no one but God could look like this. The purity and holiness continued to come forth from his face and I began to feel that purity and holiness enter into me. I wanted to get closer to see his face.

I felt no fear but rather total freedom as I moved towards him. Standing now only a few feet from him, I tried to look into the light surrounding his face but as I did he moved to one side, and as he moved all the light moved with him.

CHAPTER NINE: THE DOOR AND THE DECISION

I (Jesus) am the Door.

Anyone who enters in through me will be saved;

he will come in, he will go out, and will find pasture.

The thief comes only in order that he may

steal and may kill and may destroy.

I came that they may have life,

and have it in abundance.

I am the Good Shepherd.

The Good Shepherd lays

down his life for the sheep.

– John 10:9-11 (NASB)

Directly behind Jesus was a circular shaped opening like the tunnel I had just traveled down. Gazing out through it, I could see a whole new world opening up before me. I felt like I was standing on the edge of paradise, having a glimpse of eternity.

It was completely untouched. In front of me were green fields and meadows. The grass itself was giving off the same light and life that I had seen in the presence of God. There was no disease on the plants. It seemed as though the grass would just spring back to life if you stepped on it.

Through the centre of the meadows I could see a crystal clear stream winding its way across the landscape with trees on either bank. To my right were mountains in the distance and the sky above was blue and clear. To my left were rolling green hills and flowers, which were radiating beautiful colours.

Paradise! I knew I belonged here. I felt as though I had just been born for the first time. Every part of me knew I was home. Before me stood eternity - just one step away. As I tried to step forward into this new world Jesus stepped back into the doorway.

The Bible says that Jesus is the door and that if you come in through him, you will go in and out and find green pastures. He is the door to life. Jesus is the way, the truth and the life. No one comes to the Father but by him. He is the only way. There is only one narrow passageway that leads into his kingdom. Few find it. Most find the highway down to hell.

Jesus asked me this question "Ian, now that you have seen do you wish to return?" I thought, "Return, of course not. Why would I want to go back? Why would I want to return to the misery and hatred? No, I have nothing to return for. I have no wife or kids, no one who really loves me. You are the first person who has ever truly loved me as I am. I want to stay in your presence forever. I wish to go on in to paradise."

But he didn't move so I looked back one last time to say, "Goodbye cruel world I'm out of here!" As I did, in a clear vision right in front of the tunnel, stood my mother. As I saw her I realised my mistake; there was one person who loved me – my dear Mum. Not only had she loved me, but also I knew she had prayed for me and had tried to show me God. In my pride and arrogance I had mocked her beliefs. But she had been right after all, there was a God and a heaven and a hell.

I began to consider how selfish it would be to go through to paradise and leave my mother believing that I had gone to hell. She would have no idea that I'd made a deathbed prayer and repented of my sins and received Jesus as my Lord and Saviour. She would have just received a dead body in a box from Mauritius.

So I said, "God, there's only one person really I want to go back for and that is my mum. I want to tell her that what she believes in is true, that there is a living God, that there is a heaven and a hell, that there is a door and Jesus Christ is that door and that we can only come through him".

Then as I looked back again, I saw behind her my father, my brother and sister, my friends, and a multitude of other people. God was showing me that there were many other people who also didn't know, and would never know unless I was able to share with them. I responded, "I don't love those people" but he replied, "I love them and I desire all of them to come to know me."

Then the Lord said, "If you return you must see things in a new light." I understood that I must now see through his eyes, his eyes of love and forgiveness. I needed to see the world as he saw it – through the eyes of eternity. "God, how do I return?" I asked, "Do I have to go back through the tunnel of darkness, back into my body? How can I go back? I don't even know how I got here." He said, "Ian tilt your head... now feel liquid drain from your eyes... now open your eyes and see."

CHAPTER TEN: THE RETURN

You have rescued me from death;

you have kept my feet from slipping.

So now I can walk in your presence, O God,

in your life-giving light.

— Psalm 56:13 (NLT)

Immediately I was back in my body. My head was tilted to the right and I had one eye open. I was looking at a young Indian doctor who had my right foot elevated in his hand and was prodding a sharp instrument into the base of my foot. He was looking for any signs of life. Little did he realise that I was now alive and looking at him.

I wondered what on earth he was doing but then the penny dropped; "He thinks I'm dead!" At the same time the doctor stopped what he was doing and turned his head in the direction of my face. As our eyes made contact, terror swept over his face, as though he had just seen a ghost. Blood drained from his face and he went as white as a sheet. His feet nearly left the ground.

I was shaken by this and I asked God to give me the strength to tilt my head to the left and look out the other side. As I slowly turned my head to the left I saw nurses and orderlies in the doorway staring at me in amazement and terror. No one said a word. I apparently had been dead for some 15 to 20 minutes and was being prepared for the morgue. I felt weak and I closed my eyes but I quickly opened them again to check that I was still in my body. I wasn't sure whether or not I would disappear again.

I was still paralysed and I asked God to help me. As I prayed I felt a tingling sensation in my legs, accompanied by a comforting warmth. I continued to pray and the doctor just stood there shaking his head. The warmth spread up into my body and arms. God was healing me! I was so tired. I closed my eyes again and fell soundly asleep.

I didn't wake again until the next afternoon. When I woke I saw my friend Simon standing outside my room looking in through the window. He looked pale and was shaking his head. He couldn't believe I was alive. He had followed my trail to the hospital and had brought a New Zealand friend of mine with him. "So you had a pretty rough night aye?" this friend asked. "Yeah mate" I replied. "I don't really know what happened." I didn't want to say, "Actually – I died!" I was still coming to terms with all that had happened and didn't want them to say, "Off to the rubber room for you – you've taken too much dope and it's coming out your ear-holes!"

"This place smells like a latrine," they said. "We're getting you out of here. We'll look after you." I resisted them – I wanted to stay in the hospital but they climbed in the window, picked me up and walked me out. The doctor came and tried to physically restrain them but they pushed him out of their way.

A taxi was waiting. Simon wouldn't come in the taxi with me as he was still afraid that I was a ghost. They took me home to my bungalow on the beach and put me to bed. Then they went straight out to the living room and had a party!

I was exhausted and hungry. I went to sleep again and woke up in the middle of the night shivering and perspiring. My heart was filled with terror. I was lying facing the wall. I rolled over to see what was scaring me.

Through my mosquito netting and through the steel bars on the windows I could see seven or eight pairs of eyes looking at me. There was a light red glow to them. Instead of a round pupil they had slits like a cat. They seemed half human, half animal. I thought, "What on earth are they?" They looked into my eyes and I looked into theirs and I heard a whisper, "You're ours and we're coming back." "No you're not!" I cried. I grabbed my flashlight and shone it at them. There was nothing there - but I knew I'd seen them!

I wondered if I was going crazy. I began feeling like I might mentally snap. I had to settle myself down and convince myself I wasn't going insane. I'd been through so much in the last 24 hours. So I said, "God, what's going on?"

Then he took me moment by moment through everything I'd been through. It was as if he seared it onto my mind. At the end of this I asked him," what are these things that seem to want to attack me?" He replied, "Ian, remember the Lord's prayer". I tried to remember it with my mind again but I couldn't. Then up from my heart came all the words through to "deliver me from the evil one".

I prayed this earnestly from my heart. Then God said, "Turn the lights out Ian." I gathered up my courage and turned off the main light. I sat on the edge of my bed with my flashlight on. I felt like a Jedi warrior from Star Wars! I began thinking, "If I don't turn my flashlight out I'm going to have to spend the rest of my life sleeping with the light on." I turned the flashlight off. Nothing happened. The prayer had been effective. I lay down and went to sleep.

CHAPTER ELEVEN: SEEING IN A NEW LIGHT

Be on guard.

Stand true to what you believe.

Be courageous.

Be strong.

– 1 Corinthians 16:13 (NLT)

The next morning I got up and prepared myself breakfast. My friends came in from their morning surf and began talking to me. I began seeing that what they were saying wasn't what they were actually meaning. It confused me, as if I was hearing two different messages. I began to see through their masks.

For the first time in my life I was beginning to see things in a new light. I could see that the intents of their hearts were totally contrary to what was coming out of their mouths. It was frightening for me because I didn't know how to react to that kind of understanding. So I retreated to my bedroom, and stayed there.

That night I woke again in a cold sweat. Something nearby was scaring me. I turned my head to look and to my horror the demons I had seen last night were now in my bedroom looking at me through my mosquito net. Yet for some reason they couldn't get to me. They were intimidating me but they couldn't actually get to me.

In my heart I had a deep peace. I knew I had seen the light of God and that light was now in me. No matter how small the flame was, it was in me and they couldn't come in. But they were certainly trying to terrify me and get me back.

I grabbed my flashlight again. This time I was afraid to get out of bed to turn on the light because they were in my room. I didn't know what power they had. I flashed the light madly around the room, leaped out of bed and dashed to the light-switch. With the light safely on I fell to the floor on my knees. I battled with my mind all over again, just trying to keep my sanity. Again I prayed the Lord's Prayer and then I went back to sleep.

There were two more nights to go before I was to fly out of Mauritius to New Zealand. The next night I was woken by a tapping on my window. It was a girl saying, "Ian, I want to talk to you, let me in." As I knew the girl I thought nothing of it. Half asleep I walked to the door and unlocked it. The moment I opened the door she grabbed it and I saw her eyes. I could see the same red tinge in her eyes that I had seen in the eyes that had haunted me for the last two nights. She began to speak in word perfect English. She was Creole and had never spoken perfect English. She said, "You are coming with us tonight Ian. We are going to take you somewhere."

Then I heard other footsteps coming. I tried to pull the door closed but it was as if this girl had gained a supernatural strength and I couldn't move it. Then out of my heart came the words, "In Jesus' name – go!" She reeled backwards as if she had been punched in the chest. As I watched her recoil back up I slammed the door in her face and locked it. I was trembling, but safe for the meantime.

Finally it was my last night and I was all packed and ready to go. A taxi was coming for me at 5am. I went to sleep but was woken in the night, this time by stones hitting the window. It was the girl again. I was prepared and had locked the doors but I had left a small window open. I thought, "Whatever these creatures are, they are out to kill me and they are using humans to do it!" I was about to jump up and shut the window when a big black arm came through it and flicked the latch. I heard the girl softly saying, "Ian, we want to talk to you. Come out." I was pretending to be asleep and the stones came on the windows again. This time she was louder, "Ian, come out." Then heavier stones began coming right through the window and she was angry now, "Ian, come out!"

I turned suddenly and saw a spear coming through the open window towards me. I grabbed my flashlight. "The best form of defence is attack" I thought and I shone the flashlight into the spear wielder's eyes. There was that red tint again! I leapt up screaming for all I was worth, grabbed his spear and thrust it back at him so he loosed its hold. I threw it out the window and slammed the window shut.

Quickly I shone the flashlight outside on three men and a woman. They cowered away like dogs about to be stoned. What amazed me was how afraid of the light they were.

I was so disturbed that I stayed awake the rest of the night waiting for the taxi to come. But it never came. I woke my surfing friends and asked if they would go find the taxi for me. They found it incapacitated. Someone had thrust steel rods through its radiator in the night. It was the only taxi in town and my friend had to go to the next town to get a taxi for me there.

By the time he returned there were a group of Creole's outside my house with sticks and the driver was afraid to drive by them. Apparently I had caused quite a sensation in the town because of my miraculous recovery. The townsfolk knew I should have been dead and being a superstitious people, considered me a ghost or something worse. I managed to evade the antagonists though and made it to the airport to board my flight to New Zealand via Australia.

In Perth I caught up with my younger brother who was living there. I tried to tell him what I had seen. He was shocked and couldn't believe it. I slept in his room that night as he had left to return to New Zealand, and in the middle of the night I awoke to have white-eyed demons attacking me. I stormed out of the room to see sitting in the fireplace a small Buddha. As I looked at it God spoke to me that the white-eyed demons came out of this idol. I was amazed! Now I knew that what I had experienced with the idols in Colombo was demonic. I decided to shorten my trip to Australia and return to New Zealand immediately.

On the plane descending into Auckland, New Zealand, I asked the Lord, "What have I become?" I had my Walkman on with 'Men at Work' playing. A voice spoke over the sound of the Walkman and said, "Ian, you have become a reborn Christian." I took off my Walkman and looked around to make sure no person on the aeroplane had said it. Then I reached into my bag for my dark glasses. I put them on and in the relative seclusion that they provided I quietly freaked out. A Christian! Is that what I was? Who would want to be a Christian? It hadn't yet occurred to me that that was what I had become.

My parents picked me up from the airport. Back home, my mum had left my bedroom with its surf posters exactly as it had been two years ago. It was like walking into a time warp. I'd come home to a refuge. I went to sleep that night and was woken in the middle of the night by something shaking me. By now I knew how to get rid of the demons using the name of Jesus and the Lord's Prayer.

They had to go, but what were they doing in my bedroom, in my house? I was furious! I got up and decided to give them a verbal lashing! So I went for it! I woke my parents up but I went for it! I sat down on my bed and said, "God – I'm sick of these things harassing me in the middle of the night. What must I do to get rid of them?" He said, "Read the bible." I responded, "Next you'll be asking me to go to church! I haven't got a bible!" "Your father has a bible – go and ask him for it."

So I did. I started reading from the beginning, from the book of Genesis:"In the beginning God created the heavens and the earth. The earth was empty, a formless mass cloaked in darkness. And the Spirit of God was hovering over its surface. Then God said, "Let there be light," and there was light. And God saw that it was good. Then he separated the light from the darkness."

I wept when I read this. I'd been to university and studied all sorts of books but I've never even looked at the one book that could tell me the truth. For the next six weeks I read from Genesis to Revelation. Everything that I had seen in heaven was described in that book!

In Revelation chapter one I read about Jesus, clothed in garments of white, his face shining like the sun, with seven stars in his hand, the Alpha and the Omega, the beginning and the end. I read in John 8:12, that Jesus was the light of the world and those who come to him would no longer walk in darkness but have the light of life. I read about being born again by the Spirit of God in John chapter three. I read that by confessing my sins to God, he had forgiven me and cleansed me from my unrighteousness. I read about the new heaven and earth where there will be no more pain or crying.

I learnt that when a demon is cast out of someone it tries to come back to its dwelling place. I learnt that Jesus had given me authority over the demons I had encountered and that demons could inhabit idols. The bible inspired awe in me, as I had never realised the truth that was written in its pages was so vital for life.

Since this experience in 1982 I've been following Jesus Christ as my Lord and Saviour. Initially I spent some time on my sister's dairy farm in New Zealand getting my life sorted out. Midway through 1983 I joined YWAM (Youth With a Mission) and sailed with them around the Pacific Islands telling the people there about God's love. Then I went back into South East Asia and ministered among the unreached tribal people of Malaysia. For three years I worked in the jungles of Sarawak and the mainland peninsular. During this time I met my wife Jane.

Since then, I have worked both in the church (I am now an ordained minister), and as an itinerant speaker, travelling to many nations around the world sharing this testimony. My wife Jane and I have three beautiful children, Lisa, Michael and Sarah. Our desire is to continue sharing the amazing good news of God's unconditional love and mercy, and his provision through Jesus' death on the cross for forgiveness of our sins, to everyone we meet.

The whole story you have been reading is a true story and is based on true events. You can see the whole story in video format by clicking the link below.

Click this link to see the video!

CHAPTER TWELVE: WHAT NOW FOR YOU?

This is how much God loved the world:

He gave his Son, his one and only Son.

And this is why: so that no one need be destroyed;

By believing in him,

Anyone can have a whole and lasting life.

God didn't go to all the trouble of sending his Son

merely to point an accusing finger,

telling the world how bad it was.

He came to help,

to put the world right again.

Anyone who trusts in him is acquitted;

Anyone who refuses to trust in him has long since

been under the death penalty without knowing it.

John 3 (The Message)

God's love for us is overwhelmingly apparent. He sent his own son, Jesus, to die in our place, paying the price for our sin. The bible says that the penalty of our sin is death, and none of us are sinless, but the gift of God is eternal life through Jesus Christ (Romans 5:8–11). It is your choice – you alone can choose life for yourself!

If this book has challenged you to consider how you will respond to God's offer of life, it may be helpful for you to pray a prayer like Ian did.

* Ask God to forgive you for all your sins.

* Forgive anyone in your own life who has in any way wronged you.

* Ask God to be Lord of your life and commit yourself to following and serving his will.

If you have made the decision to follow Jesus, it will be important to find some like-minded people who can encourage you and help you to grow in your faith. Get yourself a bible and begin reading it – it may be easiest to start at the book of John (you'll find it by looking at the contents page at the beginning of the bible).

Our prayer for you is that Christ will live in you as you open the door and invite him in. And that with both feet planted firmly on love, you'll be able to take in with all Christians the extravagant dimensions of Christ's love. Reach out and experience the breadth! Test its length! Plumb the depths! Live lives full of the fullness of God! (Ephesians 3 – The Message)

NOTES

IAN'S WEBSITE

For more information on Ian and his current speaking locations, visit his website at:

www.aglimpseofeternity.org

BOX JELLYFISH

For more information on Box Jellyfish check out these websites:

http://animals.nationalgeographic.com/animals/invertebrates/box-jellyfish.html

www.outback-australia-travel-secrets.com/box-jellyfish.html

SCRIPTURE REFERENCES

You can check out how Ian's testimony lines up with what the Bible says by comparing it with these passages from the Bible:

* Death and judgement; Matt 25:31-46, Rom 2:6-11, Rom 14:7-12, 1 Cor 15:35-44, 2 Tim 4:1, Heb 9:27, Rev 20:11-15

* Jesus death for our sins; John 11:25-26, Rom 6:9-11, Rom 8:10-11; 31-35, Col 2:13-14, 1 Thess 5:10, 1 Pet 1:3-4

* Jesus the glorified Son of God; Ezek 1:26-28, Luke 9:29, John 20:19, Acts 7:55-56; Acts 9:3-5, 1 Thess 4:14, Rev 1:13-16

* Darkness and Light; Is 42:6, Matt 8:12; 22:13, Luke 2:32, John 1:4-9; 8:12, Acts 13:8-11, Rom 13:12, 2 Cor 4:6, Eph 5:8-14, 1 John 1:5; 2:8-11, Rev 21:23

* Eternal life; Ps 145:13, Eccl 12:5, Is 51:11; 60:19-20, Jer 31:3, Mark 3:29, Luke 16:9, John 3:15; 4:36, Rom 1:20, Eph 3:10,11, 2 Thess 2:16, 2 Tim 2:10, Heb 5:9; 9:15, 1 Pet 5:10, 2 Pet 1:11, Jude 21, Rev 14:6

* Heaven and hell; Matt 5:11-12; 8:12; 10:15; 18:10; 22:15; 23:15, 34-37, Luke 10:20; 15:7; 16:25; 20:36; 23:43, John 14:2, Rom 8:17, 1 Cor 15:42-51, 2 Cor 12:2-4, 2 Thess 1:9, Jude 6, Heb9: 12; 12:22-23, 1 Pet 1:4, 2 Pet 1:10-11; 2:4; 3:13, Rev 7:15; 14:13; 21:2-4, 10-27; 22:3-5,15

* The love of God; Ps 103:4, Ps 36:7, Matt 18:10, John 15:13, Rom 5:5-8, Gal 2:20, Eph 2:4-5; 3:19, 2 Thess 2:16, Titus 3:4

* Demons; Matt 8:29; 10:1; 12:24-30, Mark 1:23-24, 5:8-9, Luke 8:29; 10:17-18, 1 Cor 10:20, 1 Tim 4:1

BY DR RICHARD KENT

It is a matter of Biblical truth that when we die our spirit leaves our bodies. The most famous example of this is found in John 19:30, 'Jesus said 'It is finished' and bowing his head, he gave up his Spirit.' There is no question that Jesus died, as recorded in John 19:33. We are told that "alive in the Spirit" Jesus then preached to those who had drowned in Noah's flood (1 Peter 3;19).

In addition it seems likely to me that Paul himself had a Near Death Experience after he was stoned by Jews from Antioch and Iconium (Acts 14:19). The Jews were extremely angry with Paul for deserting the Sanhedrin and becoming a follower of Jesus. It is almost certain that they killed Paul, and this was invariably the outcome of stoning. Paul describes his own Near Death Experience as being "caught up into the third heaven" (2 Corinthians 12:2).

Finally, Dr Luke described the spirit of a dead 12-year old girl returning to her body, so that she came back to life. Jesus was called to see Jairus' daughter who had died, with the request that He should bring the girl back to life again. The story is recorded in Luke 8:53-55: 'They ridiculed him knowing that she was dead, but He put them all outside, took her by the hand and called saying, 'Little girl arise'. Then her spirit returned, and she arose immediately.' The clear teaching here is that when the little girl's spirit returned to her body, she came back to life. I believe that this is a Biblical explanation of the case of Ian McCormack, whose spirit also returned to his body after he had died.

17235618R00033

Made in the USA
San Bernardino, CA
05 December 2014